Break
Up!

DIVORCE
THE DIVORCE
AND LIVE...

ELLE A. MILLS

FOREWORD BY REVEREND JOSEPH ASMAH

Break Up!

DIVORCE THE DIVORCE AND LIVE...

ELLE A. MILLS

Printed in the United States of America
First Printing, 2021

ISBN 978-1-7364431-0-1

NyansaBa
Publishing

NyansaBa Publishing
180 Talmadge Road
IGO Bldg Suite#845
Edison NJ 08817

Dedication

This book is dedicated with love to my children Auslin, Paul and Joshua.

You have climbed my mountains, sunk into my valleys, walked my journey in your own shoes and with such grace. Your smiles, resilience, love and the hope in your eyes encourage me to cross perilous bridges and overcome my deepest fears so your hope would not drown. Thank you for keeping me going.

Acknowledgements

Father, Friend, Comforter, Keeper, Provider, Healer, Sustainer, God, my All In All.. You let me live through it to speak about it. Thank you for your mercy, grace and unfathomable love. All glory goes to You alone! Be glorified in my life and use it as you please.

Daddy, Daddy, Daddy! No words but a humble thank you. Thank you for setting the example, loving Mum (RIP) through the dark and bright days and leading us into our great spaces.I am grateful for all the sacrifices you made on my behalf. Thank you for loving and supporting me through my journey. You are my original "Risky"!

To my siblings, Mike, Livvy and Kris, " I can't able"! I love doing this thing called life with y'all! Thank you for always being there and cheering me on. Your voices sure woke me up out of some dark places!

To Reverend Joseph Asmah and Reverend Mrs. Asmah, Thank you for feeding my soul with the Word of God and for the never ending prayers. You have been there through it all and my prayer is that God will reward you immensely! To the All Nations Church, NJ.   House of Restoration Family, you rock fam! Thank you for being there for me all the way!

Contents

Foreword

The residue of divorce can be damaging, such that many people are not able to bounce back.

The subject is not easy to discuss, let alone to put it in a book because of the memories that are attached to it. The process can be so bitter and can easily make one resentful for the rest of their lives. Also, society unfortunately has a way of showing contempt on a divorced person and this easily makes many people feel disillusioned and even lose their sense of self-worth.

I was privileged to have a VIP seating in the panorama of Linda's divorce experience, and can confidently attest to the honesty and openness with which she shares her story and the lessons she has learned. This is more of a kingdom mandate, as she rightly puts it in the book, than of any personal gain. This book was written just for you, because no matter where you are in life, there are lessons we can all learn.

I want to recommend this for everyone irrespective of the side of marriage you are at the moment. There is an old adage by our elders that says, "a person with an experience is never at the mercy of a person with an argument." The dearth of experiences that are shared in this book can help anyone navigate the marriage terrain.

To the person entering into marriage, this book must be a guide to help you build a stronger foundation for your marriage. Many people enter marriage with good reasons and aspirations, yet many come out of it with life shattering experiences.

To those in marriage, please remember that good marriages don't just happen. The Apostle Paul said in 1 Corinthians 10:12 that, "Therefore, let him who thinks he stands take heed lest he fall."

To the one contemplating an exit, read the pages of this book carefully. I strongly recommend that you painstakingly consider all the things mentioned to help shape and inform your decision.

I am excited about the many lives this book will impact. This is a book in season! There are many people who have given up on life because of divorce. Many people committed suicide, others have not been able to move on in life and live every day in resentment. Read "Break Up" and pick up a copy for a friend.

Thank you, Elle Mills for becoming vulnerable for the enlightenment of many. This is definitely an excellent piece of work.

Quotes

"The terrain has no obligation to offer comfort for your peace. It offers what it is and expects that you will employ wisdom to guide your selection of the right shoes to bring along for the journey."

Elle Mills

"It is said that not all fingers are equal. The same could be said for the methodology of divorce. However, I have found out that there is, unfortunately, a reliable consistency in the output from a divorce that yields untold pain, shame, and hardship."

Elle Mills

Introduction

I am not writing to share my expert insight on divorce and how to navigate sanity after that, but to share truths I learned through my process. My journey began with the question, "Is This It?" I found myself questioning my existence in the midst of trying to find meaning to all I did. By no means was it a comfortable journey, but it was a necessary one; and there is one particularly pivotal moment that I will not forget anytime soon

It was a typical workday, and I lingered through the early morning hours of traffic on my way to work. The music was blaring in my car, as was my tradition, and I had just gone past the exit where other cars usually tried to make a fast lane change. Then it happened! I don't recall the internal dialogue, but I vividly remember the letters "MD" spoken softly into my ears. Of course, I freaked out! Wouldn't you? I started asking more questions than ever and inquired from the Holy Spirit what the letters "MD" stood for. HIS response was "Medical Doctor." The pause was long and awkward, and then I broke out in laughter. The laughter was so loud, and uncontrollable tears were rolling down my face! Here I was thinking, *I know there is greatness inside of me, BUT I AM NOT GOING TO MEDICAL SCHOOL!* At this point,

I probably made the Holy Spirit giggle. Despite my reaction, He graciously began lending context to his words explaining that Medical Doctors are healers. They apply knowledge and execute a sequence that results in healing. The trade requires long training and practice because of their impact on many lives.

He explained that similarly, divorce is such a long, tedious, and draining process that should not go to waste. Once you have gone through the journey, you have a responsibility to apply your learning to initiate and execute healing. Then He completed the explanation and said "MD, Marriage To Divorce, A Doctor Makes." This experience marked the birthing of this book, which would consume my thoughts. How I got here is by the orchestration of the Lord God Almighty!

PART 1

FRAME YOUR EXPERIENCE

"*The terrain has no obligation to offer comfort for your peace. It offers what it is and expects that you will employ wisdom to guide your selection of the right shoes to bring along for the journey.*"

Elle Mills

CHAPTER ONE

How I Got Here

ome along, my dear! Walk with me and let me explain a few things. Contrary to popular belief, divorce does not just happen. It takes a long time and gathers a collective momentum from several exclusive events of disagreement. You can use the analogy of bowling to explain it. Each roll of the ball has the potential to knock down a pin and eventually get a strike. Each pin represents many areas of marriage; sex, finances, love, communication, and so on. You witnessed each pin going down individually, but the loudest reaction is always when the collective collapse happens. You saw the makings of a divorce happening, you saw it, and you missed the opportunity to call for a time out.

The journey to the Gates of Separation and the walk into Divorce Manor takes many turns. There are many ways to explain the arrival at the Gates of Separation and the march into Divorce Manor. You have to travel a very long distance, and in that movement, you're likely to see different streets, lanes, boulevards -- what have you. The journey begins with that first step into Anger Junction, a left turn to silence strife cove and navigate begrudgingly into Retaliation Highway. Usually, at this point of the trip, Patience Terrace, Humiliation Junction, and the Rejection section of town are not far off. If you dare, you will venture into Bitter Avenue and onto Betrayal Road. It takes a lot of guts to cross over to the Reconciliation Lane, but if your motives are flawed, Breakup Corner will be right there. The only routes available at this point are usually the climb unto Crazy Hill with a dead-end staring you in the face upon arrival.

You're at an impasse staring at the finality of a divorce. It is a slow process of separation and integration into an embittered and sincerely exhausted population. The inhabitants are emotionally exhausted beings paddling murky waters and trying desperately to come up for air. Those in the water have mastered an ability to stay afloat and retain sanity, at least to the naïve eye.

DON'T KNOW WHERE BUT BE HERE!
- Elle Mills

Where is this place?
I feel lost
I feel bare
I feel a rare pang of fear

Where are you?
Where are we?
We promised this was a place
Never to journey alone
But I feel alone
Am I alone?

Where is this place?
I feel lost
I feel bare
I feel a rare pang of pain

Were we here?
Were we fair?
Were we clear?
This is not cheer!

It is not cheer!
It feels like a jeer
Oh, my God!!
Please be here!!

CHAPTER TWO

Divorce:
What Is It? (Die-vorce)

My genius idea is to change the spelling of divorce to capture the dimensional impact it has. To get to the core of what divorce is, we have to understand what marriage is. Marriage is the birth of a beautiful union, a bringing together of two souls into a three-dimensional overlap while retaining their individuality. Divorce, on the other hand, is a blunt, force trauma to the union that leaves a deep soul wound. In totality, it is simply a *successful* coup against marriage.

When something dies, there is a separation and distinctive gradual disintegration that ultimately obliterates all things good. Similarly, the finality of divorce opens a portal of death that, if left unchecked, extends its reach to destroy everything around it. The disintegration touches everything and has the potential to kill not only your spirit but your dreams, finances, love, hopes, confidence, boldness, and everything in its path.

Divorce & Death

The "D" in divorce stands for death; death of a way of life, a way of being, and participating. It can feel like a place where you go to "unbecome." Ultimately, the desperation results in a compulsive reaction to things, a dismissal, a demotion from a position of perceived security. By the end of it all, there is a lot of change that impacts your foundational boundaries. The beliefs that you have held close will shake, some truths will be disposed, and lies will fight for recognition as the perpetual influencers over your identity.

If you allow the lies to find a home in your mind, you will inevitably choose and identify with things that will pull you down. You may even uncharacteristically decide to believe that you are less than worthy, cursed, and also categorize yourself as a victim of a cruel experience. Watch out!

Outcome of Divorce

The experience leaves a bitter residue that finds solace in your despair and subtly proceeds to produce enough poison to kill you eventually.

The experience leaves a bitter residue that finds solace in your despair and subtly proceeds to produce enough poison to kill you eventually. The ensuing decay initiation can contagiously redirect your perspective, family, and whole life altogether. Does this sound scary? You bet it does! It is a frightening location, atmosphere, and existence. *Your marriage may have died, but you are alive! If you remember nothing, remember this, you do not die with the divorce.*

What You Can Do

The emotions are raw and overwhelming, and more importantly, you can't trust them to be the thing that rules your decisions at this time. Just like a seed is sown, the experience will bury you deep in the ground and cover you with dirt. You must now allow your growth through the process to help you find your outlet for existence.

The Tribe and Your Response

The friends who wait to see you crack a smile are precious and to be treasured. Your tribe of people who lend themselves to your rebirth is critical. Remember, the disintegration of marriage is so disorienting that you forget your identity. Who you are, fades into a distant memory, and the fundamental basis of your identity recuses itself into the background. For some, the marriage may have represented the totality of their identity. As such, its absence pronounces a confusion unparalleled with any other before it. It is not uncommon to struggle with the questions, *"Do I matter?"* and *"What do I do now?"*

The feeling of disorientation can only be rectified by orientation. You need someone to turn you right side up! There is a critical reminder of who you are that needs to be reinfused into your psyche to awaken you. In essence, there was an original you with a mantle or destiny before you got married. That destiny or mantle does not die with the marriage. You have to fulfill your destiny and help your seed to do the same. So, if you are the one who is to orient your children with their identity in Christ, then you are in terrible shape, if you choose to remain disoriented! If you remain disoriented, the implications for the home, community, church, the body of Christ, and the Kingdom are catastrophically far-reaching.

The catastrophe's magnitude is a broad topic for another day but let us explore this from the mothers' lens. As mothers, we forget that our children drink from our well. The fluid composition in our well is essential because not all fluid is water for growth, increase, and life. When your polluted water begins to flow, life starts slowly shrinking its territory to a parched land. The properties of the water flowing from you do not nourish. So, you see, it goes without saying, "Oh woman! You cannot afford to decay!"

It is easy to wish for rapid decay. After all, society has ill-defined the parameters of marriage to encompass the reason for living. The definition is a broad spectrum that suggests the very reason for living is all about a union. This kind of thinking is eroding the importance of individual significance vs. the wife's purpose. Marriage has become the definition of existence, and outside of it, purpose has lost its meaning. Let's pause and think about it for a second.

I believe that God, in His immense and unfathomable wisdom, created each one of us. He did so with a unique purpose defined before we were formed. This truth means that you and I are more than our marital status and we are equipped with the pre-existing capability for our journey on earth. Consequently, it takes a recognition of both truths to reorient yourself fully. Once you grasp these, you can choose to execute your Kingdom mandate and come into full existence as a child of God. Granted, you are going through something devastating, but I caution you to recognize it for what it is. Change your language to *"I am growing through this!"* and embrace your processing for your progress.

You've probably realized by now that I have traveled this terrain and gleaned a thing or two about the thorns, stones, and thickets that define this dry path. You are right! There are five stones that I picked up on my journey to the Divorce Manor, and I have confirmed their value. I will let you in on each learning phase and I sincerely hope that you will employ my ladder as your elevator to accelerate through the stops on this grueling terrain.

REFLECTIONS

1. What has changed?
2. What has not changed?
3. Where am I and where do I need to be?
4. How will I get there?

LESSON 1: Divorce Disrupts

One of the first stones I abruptly stepped on was the Disruption Stone. Its sharp edge rendered a deep penetration into the sole of my foot and initiated the slow bleeding. As I bled, I felt like I was watching my dreams increase their distance from my grasp. This disruption was not in alignment with my plan. I bet you have life plans too?! Well, many are the plans of a man, but life happens! I had ideas, dreams and fantasies; yes, stories that I was waiting for time to unveil! I dreamt of the picket fence with the kids running in the backyard and living the perfect married life that most couples dream about. I thought we had love and believed that it was enough to sustain the union. I came to find out that I may have been riding on this idea for a little too long.

"The thief comes only to steal and kill and destroy;
I have come that they may have life and have it to
the full."

John 10:10 [NIV]

LESSON 2: Divorce Deceives

I found stone number two not too far off. It was a uniquely shaped stone and captured my attention for a while. I thought it looked beautiful, but its beauty was deceitful and soon revealed when I picked it up and turned it upside down. There it was, the Stone of Deceit. The moist soil beneath it was harboring all kinds of worms and insects. I thought I was taking this with me as a keepsake, but I quickly set it down. Deceit is the entrapment that divorce ushers in, and it runs deep. When you look at divorce from within the marriage walls, it resembles and promises freedom. In reality, it is just fortified confinement with little promise of freedom. You are trapped in a false dimension of beliefs about yourself, your worth, and your purpose, and it stagnates the achievement of your vision. Soon enough, you will begin adopting these falsehoods as your truth. Be warned, because staying in this place called "deceit" will destroy you! Be reminded that "to deceive" is to cause (someone) to believe something that is not true, typically to gain some personal advantage. The word which is derived from the Latin "decipere" means to trap, catch, or cheat. I particularly appreciate the Latin definition, which describes deception's nature as an intentional ensnaring or trapping. The enemy is out to trap you, so checkmate!

LESSON 3: Divorce Destroys

Stone number three did not disappoint. The stone looked beautiful on the outside, but as I picked it up, it crumbled. The surface looked like a stone, but the consistency was that of sand. The disruption had gained my attention long enough to adopt the deception into my operation norms. It was now pulling down all my pillars of belief, trust, and hope. Destruction was slowly making my life its home and destroying it slowly. The outlook on my dreams and vision became poisoned with the suggestions volunteered during my internal dialogue.

I recall this stage vividly and remember being offended by the most insignificant comments by those around me. My concept of self was utterly crushed. Any attempted complimentary remarks were met with disbelief and utter irritation because each begged the question, *"If I was oh so great, why did my husband leave?"* The little confidence, joy, hope, and trust remaining was entirely shattered!

I would love to assure you that all of this happens in isolation. The unfortunate truth is that the fruit from this stage, if unmanaged, will spill over into all aspects of your life. The emotional turmoil will begin a process of permanency. Roots will quickly form and coil around all positive reminders and remainders. Deep-seated feelings of unforgiveness and bitterness will find expression and will confidently throw cold punches at all incoming positive matter. It is a slow process of degeneration and disintegration.

LESSON 4: Divorce Steals

Despite my best efforts, I could not find stone number four. I had lost what was familiar, secure, anchoring, and nourishing. I was empty, and if you could name it, I had lost it! The enemy was taking it all, every last bit. There was now a loud absence of peace, joy, trust, hope, and anything comforting you could think of. I became an empty shell, cruising through life on autopilot with no regard for consequence. The cruising took me to unfamiliar places and through frightening experiences. If you find yourself at this stage, I caution you to be very careful. Extreme caution is the best response to all that is unfolding.

LESSON 5: Divorce Kills

The last stone was sharp-edged and needed a cautious strategy to pick it up. I walked around it in contemplation and finally picked it up carefully to observe it in full spectrum. It had holes and looked cracked on some sides. It was moist on the outside, had crevices filled with worms and dirt. It felt like looking at a reflection of my heart. I could hear the echoes, words sobbing uncontrollably. All it said was, "*I'm all done and burnt out with nothing left.*" The lies had gained root and sucked dry my will, purpose, and hope. I now resigned myself just to sit and wait for the final disfigurement and contemplated dropping everything and letting go. The pity ballad was at its loudest and demanded my attention even amid the counsel of godly friends, acquaintances, and unsolicited advisers. I felt like they were a herd of naysayers who were out to disrupt my demolition party! Their distant call to wake up from the place of doom was faint, and the noise of destruction screamed at me, requesting a response to eternal ruin. The sirens were blaring, and the pleas were silently pouring in from all to reconsider my resolve. It was in their words, looks, and stares and specific in their hugs.

LETTING GO
- Elle Mills

Yes, it did happen!
The two sides of the story
Commentary volunteered
The deep toxic seeds of unforgiveness
The wrenching disappointment
The displaced confidence
It happened. Yes, it did happen!

But why it happened
is not for wrapping
In select assumptions
Let it settle in its achievement
Let it reveal its desire
Let it release its venom
Or else there is no desire
To heal the toxic pain and canker.

It happened
Yes, it happened!
But it found me, to allow me
To happen how I am supposed to happen.

Yes! It did happen and,
I am happening because it happened.

My Stone Wall

I gathered five unique stones, and from this collection, I understood many things. Every human being is born an individual and whole. You grow up through a multitude of experiences that shape you into a version of yourself. If marriage happens, it introduces a person into the equation. The hope is that the union will reiterate the strength of two cords. A dependence forges, and a strong and robust shared identity emerges. When divorce strikes, you witness the separation of these whole beings that came together as one. For as long as the individuals see the other party as essential to their "wholeness," they will continue to pursue their return to validate their perceived identity.

For as long as the individuals see the other party as essential to their "wholeness," they will continue " *to pursue their return to validate their perceived identity.*

However, the flaw in this perception is that the other person made them whole versus God, making them complete through Christ. Ultimately, this is a decision point that informs the acceleration of the re-orientation process. If you can see that Christ makes you whole, the brain can begin to readjust its execution sequence to operate as a complete unit. It can proceed without waiting for additional reinforcement. Because it has all the resources needed to work, the ignition response is instant and swift. There is no longer a lag for other participants.

On the other hand, if you insist that the other party's inclusion is what makes you whole, then you adjust to a position of pause. You are essentially waiting for the other person's return because you believe that you cannot exist without them. This mindset is an automatic invitation to stagnation to come in and stall your purpose. It is a dangerous, irresponsible, and expensive place to elect as a residence. A quick evacuation will serve you well.

Don't let this experience kill your zeal for life but rather let this fuel your resolve. The dimension of divorce is a territory that questions your purpose and undermines your God-given capacity to achieve significance. Once you enter this dimension, confusion is a familiar companion. The blame pendulum swings to and fro, pursuit's directing weights that ensure stagnancy. There is a whirlpool that steadily forms, and it draws its strength, speed, and relevance from your retained association with divorce. The unfavorable identity you have of yourself is now its fuel. In my experience, I found this terrain to be harsh, painful, and unforgiving. Do not stay in this dimension so long that you promote it to a realm and settle there.

I lingered in the dimension of divorce a little too long, in my opinion. While I remained, I employed different faces, and I mastered them as a defense mechanism against all things external. There were many faces; angry, bitter, strong, hurt, painful, kill, suck it up, smile, clueless, zoned out, and my favorite, which I felt was consistently demanded by the church, the "it is well" face. All my life's doubts and insecurities now flocked to the experience to find meaning, relevance, and to secure their existence. My repeated internal dialogue exerted its reasoning to permit every untruth to become packaged as my truth.

When I got to this point, it took the grace of God to navigate to freedom. I had to succumb to the urgent bell ringing in my spirit, demanding a response. I had to wake up recognizing the situation for what it was, a trial concealed by the social nametag divorce. The processing was long, grueling, and challenging, but eventually, this too would pass.

Take some time to reflect on your journey and the mental overhaul, physical adjustment, and emotional tuning you have to make. Here are some thought starters to reflect on dealing with the new you:

REFLECTION	YOUR RESPONSE
What was going on for you that you feel divorce has disrupted?	
What dreams have been destroyed?	
What beliefs or values have been shifted or destroyed?	
I feel the divorce experience has stolen_____ from me.	
I feel the divorce has killed _____	

As you sort through the feelings above, you will get more clarity to explore the questions below.

REFLECTIONS

1. Have you given yourself a moment to identify your location and the new demands it will make of you?
   - *Know your location and understand that you will have to adjust quickly.*
2. What is real, and what is not?
3. What have you employed as your defense mechanism?
4. How are you nurturing your mental and physical well-being?
   - *Know your triggers and allow yourself time to de-stress daily*
5. Have you located your support group/system? Who is your confidante?
   - *Be prepared to lose friends.*
   - *Be mindful of the social label landmine.*
6. How are you going to deal with limited finances?
7. How are you making sure that you seek God daily for direction, love, and peace of mind?
   - *Allow the Holy Spirit to cradle you in His peace daily.*

CHAPTER THREE

Interruption

This interruption is your time. Precious time! The pause is here, and you have to leverage it to pivot to the next phase. Divorce is a coup against unity and an interruption, plain and simple. Webster's Dictionary describes an interruption as "the stop of continuous progress of (an activity or process) or to break the continuity of (a line or surface)." The definition underscores the halt of something that should flow from a beginning to an end. If there is an interruption, that means there is still a destination. The existence of a destination is also an affirmation of a choice of pursuit. Whichever way you look at it, you have been interrupted and are disoriented.

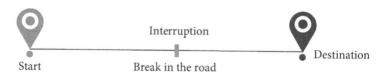

There are two kinds of interruptions: disruptive and constructive.

DISRUPTIVE INTERRUPTION

The disruptive interruption is sustained for an extended period and does not allow the opportunity for continuity. This disruption is a break that is considered an end and hijacks all efforts to move forward. You are disoriented and stagnant.

CONSTRUCTIVE INTERRUPTION

The other is a constructive interruption. This kind is momentary and allows for an assessment and a reconfiguration for the process to continue into completion. In this interruption, there is a quick rebound to get back on course. The destination is still in your purview, and the commitment to close the gap is alive.

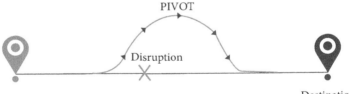

The question is, how will you choose to categorize your interruption? You have a choice to make because your continued pursuit (or not continuing) will depend on this. Your options are to either harness the chaos in the constructive interruption to propel you forward, or to allow the chaos of the disruptive interruption to sustain its significance. If you do not make a choice, it will confound and disorient you from what tomorrow holds. The choice is ultimately yours, and you have to execute with intent and commitment.

Your choice will be the catalyst for continuity. The healing journey is a long one and takes many turns, some seemingly sudden and unfavorable. The most significant challenge I know is at this stage of disorientation. My analogy looks at the setting of a village. The journey will inevitably take you through "the village." I call it a village because it is deceitfully welcoming, close-knit and comfortable. The Disorientation Village will coax you to set your bags down and stay a while. That will be a mistake because it will become an eternal stall. All the people there are like you, so they speak your language and make you feel very comfortable. Let me caution against putting your luggage down.

The thing about this village is that most people here were interrupted, came through, stayed a while, and forgot their intended destination. Once they got comfortable, they stayed in their disoriented state and allowed it to inform the rest of their lives. So, their response to life became, "I cannot do it because I went through a painful experience, and I am still recovering." They stay to eternally lick their wounds. Keep moving through the town square towards the exit gate while politely acknowledging and responding to the greetings and invitations.

Hopefully, when you unlock your pursuit's direction, it is a direction informed by the constructive interruption. If it is, challenge yourself to examine your life and your perspective. Initiate the process of unpacking and repackaging your experiences to inform your education and learning. The process is a prime catalyst for reorientation!

What do you have?

For some, this will mean learning to do many things for yourself. You have your head, heart, and your will. Let your resilience drive you like an unapologetic bull. Get up and figure it out. Do not volunteer to unleash the enemy's plan and execute it on his behalf. No, don't do that! If you have children, then you must understand this. Do what needs to be done! Know the path forward undoubtedly. Quickly internalize the fact that you cannot afford to drop the ball. Charge ahead and embrace your independence as a badge of honor, understanding the source of your strength is God Almighty.

What do you need?

You need mental, physical, and spiritual strength, divine wisdom, and undoubtedly a Godly group of people to be your support system. I call them the tribe. You need divine intervention. The temptation is to drown yourself in something or anything, but please don't do that. You do not need to get into a relationship with another man or woman to mask your tears. You do not need a drink to usher you into oblivion; neither do you need to hide in a habit. Seek God and seek Him quickly and urgently! Remember, there is an opportunity to wait too long at every stage of the process.

What do you have to preserve?

The costliest response you can have to adversity is oblivion.

Your very existence is at stake! You have your sanity to preserve because the voices are many! There are many voices inside that will demand you to do harmful things. This experience is also a battlefield. Think about it this way; nobody goes to battle and whines while fighting on the battlefield. That momentary whining can steal time at the cost of learning new things and tweaking the strategy to be applied. The costliest response you can have to adversity is oblivion. It is in your best interest to fight back, or you risk death. Vanquish or be vanquished.

Multiple battles are happening that you wish were otherwise. Unfortunately, the physical and the spiritual are simultaneous and in juxtaposition and demand you to war fiercely. Let me pause here to acknowledge that you

> *We are all someone's prey at some point. But when you are the prey, pray and fight back!*

are likely exhausted and gasping for air but realize that the tenacity for life drives us beyond our perceived ability. We are all someone's prey at some point. But when you are the prey, pray and fight back! And that my friend, is the terrain for divorcees.

HELLO SELF, LET'S HAVE A TALK

1. I know you entered the "village". Did you leave yet?
2. If not, why are you still there?
3. Are you ready to head to the exit?
4. Are you willing to do what needs to be done to get on track?

THE EQUATION IS THE STORY

There is an equation for success that originated from the combination defined by God. Any other combination results in an unedifying union that does not yield the fullness of God.

I reflected on my unsuccessful marriage through this lens to see which Equation I had lived.

The Original Equation

God created one man and gave him one woman. The man is the Visionary assigned to lead the family as the head and the priest. God gave him instructions for leadership and governance over the family. In turn, He created the woman from the man's rib and gave her the mandate of assistance and help to the man's vision articulated by God. Honoring this combination amplifies the dimension of God's participation in the family. The building blocks are inherently aligned to release Kingdom blessings. So, you have one Visionary, and one Helper to proceed in unity towards a common goal. So, the Equation below would apply:

EQUATION 1:

$$\frac{1 \text{ Vision}}{1 \text{ Helper}} = \text{Kingdom Alignment \& Advancement}$$

The Second Equation

The second Equation assumes an introduction of a second Visionary in combination with a sole Helper. This example would most likely describe where you have a woman trying to help bring two visions into fruition, one being other than her husband. This different vision could be that of an individual who has an influence equal to or greater than the husband. This Equation breeds confusion. If God gave the man a vision to lead the family forward, then the foreign participant is also presenting another idea for the Helper to support. How do you help two ideas with a deep and full commitment without breeding confusion? Consequently, the level of God's participation is limited, and the alignment with the Kingdom for the release of the blessing is compromised.

EQUATION 2:

$$\frac{2 \text{ Visions}}{1 \text{ Helper}} = \text{Confusion}$$

The Third Equation

The third combination employs one Visionary and two helpers. This situation suggests that an impostor is operating in the union. The unassigned Helper becomes a disruptive supply to the marriage God intended. The impostor will provide "help" that will contradict the "Helper" that God originally approved. The impostor is undoubtedly a fraud and can steer you into a version of the vision that does not glorify God even in its completion. I always wondered what the Visionary would be leading and governing when he has his eyes looking in two different directions. There is no way he will have a full commitment.

EQUATION 3:

$$\frac{1 \text{ Vision}}{2 \text{ Helpers}} = \text{Confusion \& Fraud}$$

The Fourth Equation

Every vision needs a helper. You may be working toward it, and that is a good thing. Know without a doubt that the selection is critical and consequential not only for your life but for your purpose, for God's approval, and for divine alignment to release Kingdom endorsement and blessing. He who finds a wife finds a good thing. The Equation below reflects the journey.

EQUATION FOUR:

$$\frac{1 \text{ Vision}}{0 \text{ Helper}} = \text{Delayed Establishment \& Manifestation}$$

There are some who may choose not to get married and for them, the Lord Himself is the Helper in all.

The Fifth Equation

This combination requires the grace of God and suggests the Visionary existed at some point in time and decided to exit. The Visionary's abandonment of the Helper has the Helper attempting to carry the vision for the family, which is an overwhelming responsibility to bear. Pulling double duty is draining and limiting. Operating on the fray of the idea and stumbling on reference points for advancement is problematic. The situation is not ideal, but while the prospects initially look weak, it is possible to employ resilience to drive the process to yield its best possible outcome.

I always thought that my life was in my ex-husband's hands. When he left, I expected everything to collapse, but it didn't, and I understood that God had me all along!

EQUATION 5:

$$\frac{0 \text{ Vision}}{1 \text{ Helper}} = \text{Delayed Implementation \& Manifestation}$$

I lived equation #5. It is hard to admit, but it is true. Somehow, given the circumstance of our coming together, I always thought that my life was in my ex-husband's hands. When he left, I expected everything to collapse, but it didn't, and I understood that God had me all along!

The Equation Summary

Equation 1	$\dfrac{1 \text{ Vision}}{1 \text{ Helper}}$	Kingdom Alignment & Advancement
Equation 2	$\dfrac{2 \text{ Visions}}{1 \text{ Helper}}$	Confusion
Equation 3	$\dfrac{1 \text{ Vision}}{2 \text{ Helpers}}$	Confusion & Fraud
Equation 4	$\dfrac{1 \text{ Vision}}{0 \text{ Helper}}$	Delayed Establishment & Manifestation
Equation 5	$\dfrac{0 \text{ Vision}}{1 \text{ Helper}}$	Delayed Implementation & Manifestation

PART 2

REFLECT TO ORIENT

"For everything there is a season, and a time for every matter under heaven: a time to be born, and a time to die; a time to plant, and a time to pluck up what is planted; a time to kill, and a time to heal; a time to break down, and a time to build up; a time to weep, and a time to laugh; a time to mourn, and a time to dance; a time to cast away stones, and a time to gather stones together; a time to embrace, and a time to refrain from embracing; a time to seek, and a time to lose; a time to keep, and a time to cast away; a time to tear, and a time to sew; a time to keep silence, and a time to speak; a time to love, and a time to hate; a time for war, and a time for peace."

Ecclesisates 3:1-22 [ESV]

CHAPTER FOUR

Identity

I n life, I have found that access requires verification and proof of identification to qualify your level of permission to a benefit. The entry demands an ID. Your uncertainty about your identity undermines access to some spaces and places. You are then inaccurately shut out from what is rightfully yours.

I can tell you this for sure! I had many questions after my divorce. I wondered about who I was now that the covering of the man was gone. My foundational understanding was that without him, I was purposeless. Unfortunately, I had internalized several subtle societal and traditional messages about the purpose of marriage. I had an identity crisis, and the question "Who am I?" needed an urgent response. After my divorce, I had managed to adopt an identity that was directly opposed to what I imagined God had in mind. In my quest for truth, I uncovered some fundamentally misunderstood anchors.

> *Your uncertainty about your identity undermines access to some spaces and places. You are then inaccurately shut out from what is rightfully yours.*

The truth is, there is a consequence for the assumption of an identity other than what our heavenly Father intended.

Picking up this alternate identity delays your purpose. You begin to hide, lie, and in the process, you open a door of deception. Who you are and who you have become initiates a vigorous war for recognition. You scheme like a Jacob, and your credibility loses its significance.

> *"So he went to his father and said, "My father." And he said, "Here I am. Who are you, my son?" Jacob said to his Father, "I am Esau your firstborn; I have done just as you told me; please arise, sit and eat of my game, that your soul may bless me."*

Genesis 27:18-19 [NKJV]

Food for thought at this point is this; the price for remaining in this alternate persona is steep. It may temporarily feel like the right benefits package, but you will soon find that it is not worth your hesitation to change. Wake Up! You are bound in your mind, and you need to stop enjoying your victimhood and break out.

Wake Up! You are bound in your mind, and you need to stop ❝ enjoying your victimhood and break out

My Discovery

> *"And the LORD God said, "[It is] not good that man should be alone; I will make him a helper comparable to him."*

Genesis 2:18 [NKJV]

I desperately wanted to discover my identity to anchor my purpose and reason for living. I was slipping slowly into a misconception about my existence, and the case for life was fading.

I went looking everywhere, meaningful, and meaningless. I searched for years, and my questions took me back to the beginning and how God created the woman.

Curiosity drove my questions, and I wondered why God used the man's rib to create the woman. Of course, I searched and discovered that the rib cage has three crucial functions: *protection, support,* and *respiration.* It encloses and protects the heart and lungs. It provides a strong framework onto which the shoulder girdle's muscles, chest, upper abdomen, and back can attach. It is flexible and can expand and contract by the action of the muscles of respiration. My response to this discovery was simply, "Wow!" I unpacked it to help solidify my understanding. The sad realization was that I did not recall pausing to understand this before I got married.

Protect and Support

This frame upholds the essential cavity's entirety and its components that support a human being's mechanism.

While the essentials are individually significant, they must be contained and positioned collectively to implement their purpose. You are an essential partner who positions, protects, and champions the man's vision and supports his execution. You are a necessary participant in his success, and you hold it all together.

Before marriage, both the man and woman are the fruit of this manifestation of God's plan when they are still with their parents and unmarried. When they each leave home, they are now vessels for the establishment, implementation, and manifestation. The newly established vision in the union and her participation as a helper protects and supports its expression.

> *"Therefore, a man shall leave his father and his mother and hold fast to his wife, and they shall become one flesh."*
>
> **Genesis 2:24 [KJV]**

Enclose And Protect The Heart And Lungs

The heart and lungs depend on the ribcage to position it to function effectively. Without the ribcage, it will work but not be as effective. Consequently, it minimizes the intended interface with an impact on the rest of the body.

Strong Framework

The rib cage is a strong framework that holds the shoulder girdle's muscles, chest, upper abdomen, and back can attach. This framework further expands the dependence on the rib cage to hold these essential components in place. As a woman, you are a custodian of precious elements that sustain the totality of the man. You are the primary support and influence the rest of the body's interaction with the body's critical components.

Flex, Expand And Contract

It is flexible and can expand and contract by the action of the muscles of respiration. The woman can extend herself to accommodate the expansion and contraction to contain the shortfall from any deflation. In support of his vision, she does all these things.

> *"The heart of her husband safely trusts her; So he will have no lack of gain."*
>
> **Proverbs 31:11 [NKJV]**

As a woman, the space you influence in a man's life is profound. According to the Scripture above, his heart "safely" trusts you. There is a relinquishing of power to you. His heart, where identity and emotion flow from, trust you to have its best interest at heart - to orchestrate, to nurture and to support.

The manner of trust is in safety. The man preserves the woman's physical security, and she, in turn, protects his emotional safety. The Bible says in Proverbs 23:7 that "For as a man thinketh, so is he…" Her words protect the fluctuations of his imagination and seek validation and significance in her language. He trusts her to treasure his dream for them. The kind of trust he has in her will not make him vulnerable but rather nurture him because she will give to him and not take away. There is much solace gained in attaining this level of trust. She is nurturing and prudent with a discerning heart. She gets him, and her speech presents him with his worth. She is the enclosure protecting his heart and lungs.

While she wields all this power and influence, the ribs are useless without the cavity components. All the expansion and contractions are contingent upon and respond to the heart and lungs in its cavity. So, there is apparent interdependence. This sequence illustrates one of the concepts behind oneness, when the two come together as one. The codependence suggests a measure of equality. Now that they are one, God has charged them to be fruitful, multiply, and have dominion; and it is all done in partnership.

The Helper

I pressed further and wondered about the woman's reference as a "Helper." What capacity and level of participation does a Helper's role entail? I found "Ezer," a Hebrew word for "Helper." Contrary to popular belief, the term "Helper" does not mean "servant." It is instead a term also used for God sixteen of the twenty-one times it appears in the 21 verses in the Hebrew concordance of the KJV, Old Testament of the Bible. The word is about God as Helper of Israel, and Warrior. It is also used in the New Testament by Jesus to describe the Holy Spirit as the Helper. Why is this important? Well, it is critical to grasp this dimension of our existence. Women are essential!

The man was created first and given a governmental mandate by God. His is to execute the vision God entrusted to him. However, take note that "something" was missing before God introduced the woman into the picture.

When God created the woman, it was a choice to provide a Helper who would be an essential participant in executing the purpose He had entrusted to Man. So essentially, we have Man the Visionary and woman the Helper. The two drive the implementation to unlock a combination key for Kingdom greatness and expansion. They are created as a force to reckon with and to be pillars for Kingdom establishment, manifestation, and dominion.

I think, as women, we should anchor ourselves in this, as this is a very critical understanding. As a woman, your degree and dimension of impact are far-reaching. Marriage is a Kingdom platform where you play a role in an assignment to ensure Kingdom alignment and expansion. Given the woman's proportion of influence, I find it interesting that the serpent went to the woman and not the man to set his plan in motion. A woman is a catalyst, architect, enforcer, and a powerful influencer in the Kingdom.

The comprehension of this identity is essential and will influence how you live your life. With that said, I encourage you to kindly spend time to get well acquainted with your purpose before marriage.

Helper -"Ezer" Reference Map

Genesis 2:18	And the LORD God said, It is not good that the man should be alone; I will make him an help meet for him.
Genesis 2:20	And Adam gave names to all cattle, and to the fowl of the air, and to every beast of the field; but for Adam there was not found an help meet for him.
Exodus 18:4	And the name of the other was Eliezer; for the God of my father, said he, was mine help, and delivered me from the sword of Pharaoh
Deuteronomy 33:7	And this is the blessing of Judah: and he said, Hear, LORD, the voice of Judah, and bring him unto his people: let his hands be sufficient for him; and be thou an help to him from his enemies.
Deuteronomy 33:26	There is none like unto the God of Jeshurun, who rideth upon the heaven in thy help, and in his excellency on the sky.
Deuteronomy 33:29	Happy art thou, O Israel: who is like unto thee, O people saved by the LORD, the shield of thy help, and who is the sword of thy excellency! and thine enemies shall be found liars unto thee; and thou shalt tread upon their high places.
Psalm 20:2	Send thee help from the sanctuary, and strengthen thee out of Zion;
Psalm 33:20	Our soul waiteth for the LORD: he is our help and our shield.

Psalm 70:5	But I am poor and needy: make haste unto me, O God: thou art my help and my deliverer; O LORD, make no tarrying.
Psalm 89:19	Then thou spakest in vision to thy holy one, and saidst, I have laid help upon one that is mighty; I have exalted one chosen out of the people
Psalm 115:9	O Israel, trust thou in the LORD: he is their help and their shield.
Psalm 115:10	O house of Aaron, trust in the LORD: he is their help H5828 and their shield
Psalm 115:11	O house of Aaron, trust in the LORD: he is their help and their shield.
Psalm 121:1	[[A Song of degrees.]] I will lift up mine eyes unto the hills, from whence cometh my help.
Psalm 121:2	My help cometh from the LORD, which made heaven and earth.
Psalm 124:8	Our help is in the name of the LORD, who made heaven and earth
Psalm 146:5	Happy is he that hath the God of Jacob for his help, whose hope is in the LORD his God:
Isaiah 30:5	They were all ashamed of a people that could not profit them, nor be an help nor profit, but a shame, and also a reproach.
Ezekiel 12:14	And I will scatter toward every wind all that are about him to help him, and all his bands; and I will draw out the sword after them

| Daniel 11:34 | Now when they shall fall, they shall be holpen with a little help: but many shall cleave to them with flatteries. |
| Hosea 13:9 | O Israel, thou hast destroyed thyself; but in me is thine help. |

Why Put Up A Fight?

It is clearly understandable, and straightforward. One of the most severe cases of identity theft is divorce. There has been an unnatural shift and alteration of God's course and assigned purpose for mankind. The divorce experience has stolen your identity and compromised your life's purpose. You are fighting to restore, and recover all that was taken from you so you can live your fullest life. Before the experience, there was no limit nor boundary to your dreams. So, why allow this interruption to rewrite the script? Don't let the funk deposit no junk! After all, it is an event and not a cycle. So, make sure your response sequence matches just that, an event!

> One of the most severe cases of identity theft is divorce.

> Before the experience, there was no limit nor boundary to your dreams. So, why allow this interruption to rewrite the script? Don't let the funk deposit no junk! After all, it is an event and not a cycle. So, make sure your response sequence matches just that, an event!

Traditionally, the sequence of our actions after divorce suggests finality and not continuity. But, there is an error in living life after divorce as if it were the end of the totality of your being or existence. There is a correction necessary, and it resides in remembering that marriage was never the beginning. The temporary pause button is not to replace the finish whistle/horn.

I remember this period well. The Holy Spirit initiated a process of awakening, orienting, and teaching about the life I was to lead and how marriage fits into the eternal equation. My life's journey was never solely a marriage journey but a Kingdom journey. What seemed like a challenge was instead a different route to learning and a pivot to more incredible things. It was clear that the experience was to eliminate me.

However, my adversity was now a route for my redemption, and God was using my processing for my progress. With this new understanding came the onset of the realization that while marriage is a good thing, its ending, or dissolution, was not the mark of the end of my life's purpose. I understood that I was created and oriented with my God-given purpose and my Kingdom journey. It was clear that the earth had been waiting for me to deliver on my God-given purpose, which is to fulfill my destiny. It may have taken a while, but I eventually realized that the direction of my life is orchestrated by HIM to achieve that purpose. All the "assets" God entrusted to me must yield a profit, and I had to wake up to invest, market, and account for the ROI (Return On Investment). The clarity put a hop in my step, and it was a revelation and rejuvenation like no other!

The life journey was always a Kingdom journey and never a marriage journey! I had never thought of that, and it definitely was not apparent at the time, but I now retain it with effusive clarity. Come to think of it; the life we are to live was always to fulfill the Kingdom's purpose. I am to live a very precious well-orchestrated, and purposeful life. While predetermined, the execution was subject to my choices and paths of alignment.

REFLECTIONS

1. Who are you?
    *   Through your lens
    *   Through God's lens
2. How does marriage fit into your Kingdom Journey?
3. What assets has God entrusted to you?
4. What have you done with the assets?
5. What questions do you still have about your identity?

CHAPTER FIVE

Orientation: Right Side Up

To the one reading about these experiences, lend me your attention for a tête-à-tête. There is a surprisingly sizable demographic existence of deeply exhausted women who are acutely disoriented from the divorce experience. Unfortunately, they remain busy presenting themselves as victims! Because this population invests in disorientation, they have no stability and make no progress in living their Kingdom journey.

Your world has been undoubtedly rocked and shaken. However, I caution you not to remain so shocked that you are eternally unable to focus. So focus must happen sooner than later. When you shake anything, after a while, it returns to its still form. Even a pendulum comes to rest at some point. When you are disoriented, it signals that you have lost something familiar. It could be a familiarity with an atmosphere, location, or even a lifestyle. The list is endless, but it has shifted your focus and altered your bearings. It may feel like flawless continuity is no longer an option for you because you are grasping for something, someone, or

> *Beware at this stage of the journey because if you anchor on to the wrong something or someone, you will sink eventually, if not immediately.*

anything familiar to anchor you. Beware at this stage of the journey because if you anchor on to the wrong something or someone, you will sink eventually, if not immediately.

Orientation With Your Circumstance

Disorientation was like quicksand. All it took was one thought after another, and I would sink deeper and deeper into a dark and empty place. I slipped so fast that I missed the speed of the eclipse of my light.

There is a lesson to be learned here. You must get oriented to your circumstance quickly and understand what arsenal you have for your warfare. Your comprehension and resilience are paramount for your survival. You are disoriented, and the familiar things are mostly gone. However, they cannot all be gone! You have cried, and for now, it is enough. Dry your tears so you can see clearly, or you risk unwelcome stagnancy.

In reflection, I can say I knew I was spiraling out of control. The jolt from disorientation came with realizing that my Kingdom journey was more connected to my divine purpose than my marital status. I was

> *The jolt from disorientation came with realizing that my Kingdom journey was more connected to my divine purpose than my marital status.*

reintroduced to myself, and thoughts about the context of life precipitated this. I had never encountered this before. The understanding was new, but somehow, along the way, I understood that I am a woman of substance, responsible for executing my purpose to the end. The processing came with an exorbitant cost too expensive to be ignored. Perhaps, the elements of character that the divorce journey demanded I confront were not pleasant, but the confrontation was necessary. The experience brought me to a place of self-confrontation and a commitment to improve myself continuously to become a better version of myself.

In my evolution, I learned not to let people referee the measure of my improvement. I found that they were acutely blind to my starting point and helplessly biased! With this, I encourage you to let the Holy Spirit be your Guide and Coach. Trust me, He will convict you, and the response will be your choice to make. There is very little room to argue about the demands at this stage. You have to get up from this place! It may feel like a knockout from the most well-thrown punch. You are winded and dazed, but honey, you need to get up! Get up now!

> *In my evolution, I learned not to let people referee the measure of my improvement. I found that they were acutely blind to my starting point and helplessly biased!*

You have to let your understanding of your identity push you back on track to pursue your purpose. Allow yourself to take stock of what has happened and how it has shifted your core. Reach deep and pull out the toxins that have been circulating to hold you hostage. The truth must prevail to unseat the lies and make way for freedom. It is time to detox from all the junk. Do the work, and you will not regret it!

> *It may feel like a knockout from the most well-thrown punch. You are winded and dazed, but honey, you need to get up! Get up now!*

"Before I formed you in the womb, I knew you,
Before you were born, I sanctified you; I ordained
you a prophet to the nations."

Jeremiah 1:5 [NKJV]

The Truth of Whose You Are

The basic understanding of who you are will drive your actions. At this point, you must grasp the concept of who and whose you are. You are a creation of God, created to nurture and manifest a Kingdom calling. God calls you, and you are His temple. He bought you with His Son's precious blood to mold you into a Kingdom participant and enforcer. This truth matters because it will shape how you think of yourself and will inform what actions flow after that. If you believe you are precious, well, your efforts will reflect the same.

On the contrary, if you think of yourself as nothing but just a chance creation, then your actions will lack direction, consistency, and resolve. If the king's daughter starts acting like a pauper's child, questions follow. Ephesians 2:10 says, "We have become his poetry, a re-created people that will fulfill the destiny he has given each of us, for we are joined to Jesus, the Anointed One. Even before we were born, God planned our destiny and the good works we would do to fulfill it!"

"As in water face reflects face, So a man's heart
reveals the man."

Proverbs 27:19 [NKJV]

As a man thinks, so he is. So, check your thinking. Let the audit reveal the gaps and read the Word of God to reacquaint yourself with who He says you are so you can reposition yourself and get back on track.

The Truth of Where You Are

Denial enforces stagnation. We only progress from where we think we are. Your physical, mental, and emotional location will play a role in where you see yourself going. Fortunately, your identified area will allow you to do the forecasting. Sometimes, out of denial, we mentally position ourselves in a better place than we truly are. That mindset does not push us to do as much work as is needed.

To move forward, you need to acknowledge that you are in unfamiliar territory, and that will allow you to assess the new terrain. When you ask the question of location, a description follows to craft a physical, emotional, and spiritual picture for your reaction. The image is multi-tiered and has intersectional commonality. Once that assessment is out of the way, proceed to perform a comparative analysis of your past and present. The outcome of this analysis will become the catalyst for what you decide to do next. The intersectionality allows the actions to flow and impact the different location. For example, a spiritual adjustment will inform your emotional and physical locations as well. Undoubtedly, recognizing where you are and saying it out loud is a very liberating experience and is worth the exercise.

The Truth of Where You Are Going

Destination begs for a purpose. It does not exist in a vacuum but is instead an answer to a goal. The challenge is that sometimes, we are so stuck in pain from where we come from that we take no time to reflect on where we are heading. The initial focus is the escape with no consideration for the future. You will find yourself on the road to somewhere because that is what roads do; they lead somewhere. But if we will just take the time to plan and ask God where we should go, we will find ourselves on the right road leading us to our destination and not a random one. He will direct and guide us to our place of purpose and peace.

"And he said to Hagar, the servant of Sarai, "(From where) have you come, and where are you going?" And she said, "I am fleeing from the presence of Sarai, my mistress."

Genesis 16:8 [LEB]

When you have heard from God concerning your destination, you have a choice to make. You already know where point A is. You now have the liberty to select a point B, either based on God's guidance or on your assumptions. Your destination is a reflection of how you choose to anchor your achievement. You were on your journey to fulfilment before the disruption. That destination is still within reach if you will listen to God's voice and follow His guidance for you. The choice is yours.

"The heart of man plans his way, but the Lord establishes his steps."

Psalm 16:9 [ESV]

"Trust in the Lord with all your heart, and do not lean on your own understanding. In all your ways acknowledge him, and he will make straight your paths."

Proverbs 3:5&6 [ESV]

"I will instruct you and teach you in the way you should go; I will counsel you with my eye upon you.."

Proverbs 32:8 [ESV]

The Truth of Who You Need

The path for the journey has been charted and needs a tribe to guide it to completion. Recognition has now liberated you to plan, and for this journey, you need your God tribe. These are individuals who will nurture you to wholeness by feeding you divine content. They will support your healing and champion your reconnection to God. They will, however, be truth-tellers, and this will not always be pleasant to you. Proverbs 18:24 says, "But there is a friend who sticks closer than a brother." These are the ones who will stick with you through soul-wrenching challenges and nurture you back to life with love and kindness. You have to master the overwhelming need to be isolated and surround yourself with such.

You need your Helper and Advocate, the Holy Spirit. He will infuse a directional companionship for sustainability. You need Him to imbue you with discernment to be liberated from the dependence on the God tribe. He will anchor you in a relationship that draws on His help for all things. The God tribe was only to shepherd you out of any negative place where you are tempted to participate in the fellowship.

> *"But the Helper, the Holy Spirit, whom the Father will send in My name, He will teach you all things, and bring to your remembrance all things that I said to you."*

John 14:26 [NKJV]

The Truth of What You Need To Do

All you need to do is follow. Follow the direction of God for your life. You are on your way to execute and manifest what He said about you. With His guidance, you are on a victory path to fulfilment. The truth is you have a lot to do! There is no excuse for stagnation. You have to propel yourself with God's Word and pivot to your place of participation on this earth. With directional guidance, the path is clear to your destination, and God will retrain you for your original plan.

Arise daughter, arise son and go forward. Pursue, overtake, and recover!

It's A Mantle Matter

"Before I formed you in the womb I knew you; Before you were born I sanctified you; I ordained you a prophet to the nations."

Jeremiah 1:5 [KJV]

My Christian faith teaches me that God has predetermined for us to carry specific and individually-assigned mantles. He made and established this decision before we ever stepped foot into anything, marriage included. It is not an elective or a negotiable situation. God has ordained us, and in our role as humans, as mothers and fathers and as women and men, there is a mantle to carry, and divorce does not negate that responsibility.

Divorce is one of the tentacles of destruction against the Kingdom. If you think about it, the family is the womb for the future. We nurture everything that we release into the future. We cultivated it at home with values and directional compasses that inform future actions. So, it is on us to sound the alarm for the following reasons.

Firstly, if the nurturing is allowed to proceed uninterrupted, it impacts the Kingdom's advancement. The enemy recognizes this Kingdom impact and uses divorce as a hack to undercut the union's effectiveness and, ultimately, the Kingdom. The enemy has deployed devices and weapons to disrupt and destroy marriages, and you cannot be ignorant of them.

The enemy has deployed devices and weapons to disrupt and destroy marriages, and you cannot be ignorant of them.

Secondly, we have to understand that you still carry the mandate even though you may have gone through a divorce. Of course, the preference is for the marriage to thrive, but if divorce unscrupulously finds a way to establish itself, then recognize that you are now a *"vision helper"*, and you have to execute. God created you to help the vision, so acknowledge that you need help to champion it now.

The vision is given to the man for the family. His inability or unwillingness to manifest the revelation does not stop the fruit from blossoming. Home is supposed to be a safe space where children can form, storm, norm, and reform before they are released into society by themselves. If you have children and experience divorce, know that the responsibility to nurture must still go on. Just because the mortal man

The vision is given to the man for the family. His inability or unwillingness to manifest the revelation does not stop the fruit from blossoming.

could not work with you does not imply that God, the Source of the seed, will not work with you. The seed came from God through the man, so if he ups and leaves, honey, go back to the Source. He still has the manual for the family!

I had to work through many questions to get this understanding solidified in my spirit. I often floated mentally to explore who I was and what could have precipitated my situation. It was a brutal and sometimes unforgiving journey compounded by external voices happy to harp on my shame. But let me confirm before going any further that I could never pinpoint what precipitated the situation. However, I found many issues that had gone unaddressed for a long time and ultimately resulted in the

Just because the mortal man could not work with you does not imply that God, the Source of the seed, will not work with you. The seed came " *from God through the man, so if he ups and leaves, honey, go back to the Source. He still has the manual for the family!*

separation and resulting divorce. I do know that, like the bowling game, there were many pins knocked down, but the totality of the collapse did not register early. You have taken a step toward orientation, and you have to confront you. You have to address all the toxicity that is rearing its head.

WHAT IS LURKING BENEATH?

There are a few elements of character that bubbled to the top through the experience. For the most part, characteristics that had remained quietly hidden in the bosom of the peace of love now woke up to harsh reality. They wanted to be paraded and duly acknowledged. The safety of love was gone, and their tone had evolved without care for their impact. This period is when the inner dialogue is likely the loudest and will generously volunteer thoughts of inadequacy, self-doubt, defeat, unforgiveness, intense fear, shame, and anxiety, to name a few. It was a rough journey, and in the process, I manifested the very worst of myself. If there was a way to wear a sign across my forehead that said "Beware," I probably would have volunteered to do so. Oh YES! Beware the subtle manifestation that coaxes you into thinking it is a singular occurrence that you will not witness again.

Surprise! "Hurt people hurt people" holds true for divorced people too! In hindsight, I realize that my storage of the Word of God, which was supposed to be my blueprint for rehabilitation and navigation in this toxic situation, was acutely diminished. My words had become contaminated, and I now employed them to be the carriers of negativity, hurting myself and those around me as well. I have heard it said and believe it to be true that hurt people hurt people. The outlet for all these emotions landed squarely on those closest to me. Now I can't help but think about how interesting it is that the party that caused the pain is not the rage recipient. Instead, the distance from my anger to my closest friends was the shortest travelled.

Perhaps the toxic gush was to derail me from the journey back to life. Anyway, at the end of all the processing, there is a mantle to be picked up. You have a cause to champion and a community to impact. Embrace the experience and ensure you have secured the anchors; the Word of God being the first, to keep you afloat. Take an acute note of this. The people who surround you in this phase are critical, so choose wisely.

Remember that even though you are hurting now, it will soon pass. You are angry now, but it will subside too. It may feel unreal or even unachievable, but I can guarantee that your morning will come. While you wait for the morning, do not attempt to deny where you are in the process because that will only lengthen the process. Pay attention to the facts, but let the truth be your guidepost. Acknowledge the hurt for what it is, let the tears run their course, but bid them an expedited adieu.

> *"For his anger endureth but a moment; in his favour is life: weeping may endure for a night, but joy cometh in the morning."*

Psalm 30:5 [KJV]

DIMENSIONS OF INFLUENCE

Hurt comes before pain. When you experience continuous pain, it means you have either experienced a series of injuries or an extraordinary and impactful event of damage. The strain is never isolated to one part of the body. When you get hurt, the pain is registered in your brain and has consequences for your whole body.

Many experiences of hurt and pain occurred before the divorce. Each encounter deposited an injury that precipitated pain and generated a wound that I nurtured for years.

One damage after another, they found each other and combined distortion and pain. My most critical question is, "What do you do with all the pain?"

A SOUL WOUND HAS FORMED

Mind, Will, and Emotions

The slow, painful tearing apart and eventual separation during a divorce precipitates a soul wound. You went looking for a soulmate and ended up with a soul wound. It has cut through the most profound places to secure the experience and its existence. Your mind, will, and emotions have all been traumatized by the experience. Let's unpack these to understand the depth and breadth of its impact.

Mind

Your brain is like a massive city with its connections. It is wired in a unique way to accommodate all the memories and experiences, and it stores all this information. It can take all those items to make connections that are then transmitted to the mind. Once the mind receives this information, it goes through the thinking process and relays it to the body for execution. So, your mind is responsible for the translation of what resides in the brain. In essence, your mindset matters because your body's performance and your life actions will follow suit.

In navigating the divorce journey, your mind is presented with an experience that challenges what it believes or held valuable. Your mind has to revisit your thinking to realign and solidify your mindset about your life.

Will

The will is the powerful and decisive pull toward the execution of good or evil. It is the execution of the computation of the data in the mind and the result. Those data points now influence your choices.

Emotions

The emotion is the feeling precipitated by the culmination of all the things that happen and the translation of where they sit in the spectrum of affection. So, your emotion could be a good one if the happening is closer to love or destructive as it distances itself from the love or like spectrum.

When you have a wound, it is treated so it can heal. Once it improves, it may or may not leave a scar. But one thing is sure, you now have an experience of the healing process that could inform someone's wound care. What you know could be someone's ticket out of a sticky, scarring situation.

Wallowing in your pain may seem like the obvious choice. It takes courage to open up the wound for treatment. You can choose to live in the dimension of pain or walk in a realm of healing.

Remember, the pain is only a temporary dome of doom that will eventually lift, so resist the permanent gloom. The pain will go away, and you will heal, but the pace of healing is absolutely up to you. There will be moments of shame and suffering from the wrenching disappointment that comes through the process. Allow yourself to feel it and deal with it. Locking your hurts and feelings away will only prolong the process. It is wise

> " *Remember, the pain is only a temporary dome of doom that will eventually lift, so resist the permanent gloom.*

to note that things locked away do not at once disappear. It lingers for a reasonable time only to eventually rear its ugly head.

The anger may make you feel powerful in a weird way but let it go. Don't justify your behavior or blame others for your plight. It will make it difficult to maintain relationships. As the anger, fear, and possibly guilt begins to seek expression, recognize that you have gone through significant trauma. Remember, trauma is what happens in us when something happens to us. Something has happened to you and something is happening in you. Allow yourself to process it.

> *Remember, trauma is what happens in us when something happens to us. Something has happened to you and something is happening in you. Allow yourself to process it.*

PART 3

RESET
TO HEAL

"Healing is a process towards rehabilitation. As pain rises to the surface, view it as an invitation. Ask God if there is something to learn and then pay attention."

Elle Mills

CHAPTER SEVEN

Heal

Why Should I Heal?

A season has come to an end, and change is inevitable. There is a changing of the guard, and you have to realize and accept that your significance transcends marriage, divorce, or any other experience. To heal a soul wound, you need soul food. Soul food feeds your mind, will, and emotions. It helps you cut through the clutter to align with God's Word and nourishes your inside for an outside glow. A wound makes you different. Like skin, once it is punctured, its characteristics change. When a cut is going through a healing process, there is so much going on under the skin that you do not see. Your insides have been open to the outside and must now be closed back up. An internal wound does you no good, and you have to heal.

The first step toward emotional healing is readiness. Are you ready to open the door? Are you ready to let in the truth? Are you ready to shine the light on the broken places? Are you ready to heal, or better yet, do you want to be healed? You can choose to make this your place of chaotic comfort, or you can pick up your bed now. The choice is ultimately yours but let me tell you why you must decide sooner than later.

Heal To Function

You are not functioning at your optimal level. Wounds hinder us and make us inefficient and ineffective. You have to heal to function correctly. That deep wound you have has corrupted the surrounding flesh, and if it does not heal, what would be normally repairable damage will instead become catastrophic. Nobody tells you this, but I have found that dysfunction almost always has an affiliation with hurt. The precipitating pain from the injury consistently undermines your ability to function with clarity and at full capacity. It suppresses your potential and stagnates your acceleration towards purpose. Without a doubt, a wound gets in the way of everything, not only physically but spiritually and emotionally.

Nobody tells you this, but I have found that dysfunction almost always has an affiliation with hurt.

Heal To Hear

Wounds cause pain and shift your focus. I have tried to remember when something cut me, and I recall being so distracted with the hurt I felt from the pain that I could not focus on anything else. I did not want to hear anything or anyone. Have you noticed how challenging it is to hear God speaking when you are drowning Him out or you are too distracted by everything around you? Distraction is easy but focus brings wholeness. Do you realize that His voice will reset you? His is the voice that calms the waters and soothes your heart. I have a recommendation for your consideration. Pull yourself up by the bootstraps and lean in to listen for God. Listen closely so that you can believe enough to pull on His Sovereignty and release your faith like a bridge to get you to what He has in mind. Wounds are so powerful that you cannot shout over them nor apply makeup over them. Like a canker, it will eat you up from the inside out. So, choose but make sure your choice is aligned with the business of repair.

Heal To Love

Love is an action, and you can only love others as much as you love yourself. This is a profound realization because you could be doing your best to love others, but it may not even register. Sometimes it is reciprocated, and at other times, it is not. Remember that love flows from within. It is evidence of an inner value system, belief, and is nurtured faith. If your insides are rotten, knotted up, or jumbled with unforgiveness and guilt, the fruit will most certainly reflect the same. That is what you will deposit into those around you, and it will not be welcome. Learn to love yourself. Unpack all the junk so you can see you.

Heal To Worship

Wounds tend to elevate its voice above normalcy. We worship in truth, and it is hard to be true when you are distracted with bitterness and anger. Your communion with God in this state can be accusatory and express ingratitude. You cannot enjoy His presence because you are holding on to something that does not attract His presence. His Spirit is drawn to a place (or a person) to bring liberty. You have to submit your cares and burdens so you can be elevated above the pain to worship. You have to shift your focus from the thing that is eating you up and focus on God. In this shift, you will find the catalyst for your healing. The change allows you to focus on God and allows Him to anchor you in who He is. The shift in focus will let you recognize that He is sovereign and will manage that pain and wound in a way that will work together for your good. It will, in turn, free you up to trust Him and just lay all the hurt at His feet. Listen, I am not saying it is easy, but it is necessary. Let's talk about how the faith patch can help you get to that place of trust.

Look at the visual above to help you understand the trust process. Ours is to live in the "in-between" space. The reality is that spending time on the outskirts will not hurry God. He has a vision of the beginning and the end. The hard part is taking the step, not knowing what He has in mind and the result. You have to let your faith patch be the bridge to get you to the "in-between" place. What matters most is what you do in that space. You should anchor yourself in His thoughts about you, His plans for you, and believe that He will cause everything to workout for your good. You just have to do your part.

Know that there is a fabric of healing that is looking for an opportunity to wrap itself around your heart. Allow it to embrace you with the softness of recovery to stop the bleeding.

I know it is challenging to trust again, but you must! If you are going to trust again, this is the best place to begin your journey. Know that there is a fabric of healing that is looking for an opportunity to wrap itself around your heart. Allow it to embrace you with the softness of recovery to stop the bleeding.

The Choice to Heal

Willingness and ability are a reservoir for manifestation. You would think the choice to heal is an easy one but it is not. You have to despise the shame and pain enough to let it pass quickly. By despising the shame you contextualize it and process through it so you can move on. You do not associate yourself so much with the guilt and pain because the longer you do, the more likely it is to become your identity.

> *Willingness and ability are a reservoir for manifestation. You would think the choice to heal is an easy one but it is not.*

You need to shed. The scars from the pain will be there as a reminder and that is alright. You have to remember that not identifying yourself with the problem does not mean it did not exist. The scars will be there to testify of the journey of a wound that had to heal. When you transition into the place of healing, the scars will be there, but the story will be focused on giving glory to God. Make the choice to heal because dwelling on the scars means you're dwelling on the pain and shame.

While you are in pain, you may feel like you are hanging on a cross – an elevated view for all to see your shame and pain. The visual of Jesus on the cross comes to mind. But, in the same elevated perspective, He was afforded an elevated view of the end. In the same way, your focus is on the thing that

God is working out for your good. The cross (the finished work) is now your trump card, so checkmate! Break the affiliation with pain because better lies ahead!

> *Break the affiliation with pain because better lies ahead!* "

When Christ was on the cross, those who came to jeer, support and everything in between were at the place of His perceived demise. They all stood facing Him and looking up at Him. There are many in a similar position in your place of perceived demise. They are facing you and looking at what is happening to your flesh when you hang on the cross in your hard place. They may make comments and point, prod and even poke. Very few will look in your eyes to catch a glimpse of what you see ahead. They may not see it but you must see it. If you look down, you will most certainly see what they see, which is disgust, misplaced pity, and hopelessness waiting to be branded as permanent. But I love this Scripture:

> *"Looking unto Jesus, the author, and finisher of our faith, who for the joy that was set before Him endured the cross, despising the shame, and has sat down at the right hand of the throne of God."*

Psalm 30:5 [KJV]

Here is what I recommend. Take time to heal after all the years you have been hurting. There are deposits of bitterness, strife, hate, regret, and all other kinds of stuff in your "tubes." These toxic deposits have to be flushed out, so that the new thoughts of wholeness, hope and stability can now burrow through and prepare for love's soothing. By the way, by "love," I am not suggesting that you will immediately go out and meet a new mate. That could potentially be the worst thing that you ever do! I am indeed saying that as you learn to love yourself and experience the love from the healthy relationships around you, you will begin to heal and restore lost faith.

These relationships help replace and replenish the toxic sap that has long claimed residence in your heart. Please note that it takes time, and that length of time depends on you. These are your chains, and you decide which ones fall off and how fast they fall off. Great caution should be taken to see through the full exit of the gunk. If there is still some gunk in the tube, it should and must come out. The question to always ponder is, will its exit impact the "one?"

How You Heal

You have to know where the wounds are so you can manage your expectations. But in your knowing, allow room for vulnerability. Bleeding is not always a bad thing and can help clean the wound out. Wounds heal from the inside out. In like manner, you have to heal on the inside so it is evident outside. Allow God to get the nasty things out: disappointment, fear, shame, anger, depression, offense, and betrayal.

As you progress in your healing, know this as well; you will heal your wounds, but you will not escape from the scars. Wound cleaning is essential for its healing, so let out the gunk to

As you progress in your healing, know this as well; ❝ you will heal your wounds, but you will not escape from the scars.

repair your heart. The scars are a testament and a journey reminder. It reiterates the magnitude of the wound and the depth of the healing. Quit covering up your imperfections because that is only a ploy for perfection. Leave the wound uncovered so it can breathe and then clean it and cover it to protect the advancement of the healing. The healing process fluctuations are merely an opportunity to pay closer attention to the root of what is trying to kill you.

> *The healing process fluctuations are merely an opportunity " to pay closer attention to the root of what is trying to kill you.*

The healing is an iteration of exchange moments. So for each time you uncover the wound, you allow a vulnerability. The progress is in the deposit of medicine that will allow it to heal. For each time the wound is opened, deposit words of affirmation from the Word of God. Speak words that counter the lies the enemy has sown. Tell yourself about who you are through God's eyes.

CHAPTER EIGHT

Hold The Torch

NASCAR (National Association for Stock Car Auto Racing) is not a traditional sport I would ever claim to understand. Something struck me as interesting, though. High-speed cars mark the race and circle an arena interjected by waving flags and pit stops. There are so many flags and so many colors! I noticed that the black and white checkered flag is waved frantically at the finish line, announcing the race's completion. I always wondered about that and thought it should be a green flag. I honestly found it counter-intuitive. So, I did a little research into NASCAR racing and discovered the following:

The flagman waves the green flag at the beginning of the race to start or restart the race. Green means go, so when a driver sees this flag, he slams on the gas pedal and takes off.

The checkered black and white flag is waved at the end, meaning that a driver has completed the last lap, crossed the finish line and/or won the race. I sat back and compared this to the divorce journey. The green flag starts the trip, but the black and white checkered flag announces the process' completion when you hang on the cross with many lessons learned, both good and challenging. When you have gone through the experience, it is important to announce your redemption and share your experiences! Let everyone know what the enemy planned and how God made it work for your good! Let the "word of your testimony" be loud and clear. Let it be an echoing sound, a warning, an encouragement, and an empowerment to many who may have taken the road that ought to be less travelled.

You may get the go-ahead to begin the journey, but that flag is not an assurance of a trouble-free experience. What remains important is the completion of the whole race and the crossing of the finish line. My takeaway? Regardless of what happens after the green flag is waved at the beginning, do not abandon the race because everyone is accepted at the finish line.

All the good, bad and ugly was always part of the journey. Your translation of the happenings will determine if it was a win or a loss. Frame it well.

Orient Yourself - G.O.F.R.E.E.

Know this; you are not lost. You are only disoriented. Disorientation is nothing but a thief of time. If it is upside down, there is a right side up. Disorientation exists to allow reorientation to have a rehabilitative voice. So, for that reason, you need to shed the gunk. You have to position yourself to

Disorientation exists to allow reorientation to have a rehabilitative voice. "

shed so you can "G.O.F.R.E.E." Lay aside the heavyweight.

The G.O.F.R.E.E framework is a catalyst for liberty. You get to contextualize the experience:

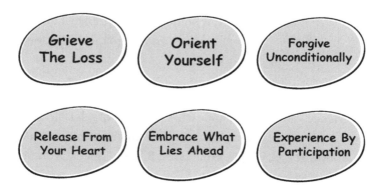

For the most part, what holds us hostage from healing is self. We lie to ourselves about what is going on because we do not want to address what we are doing wrong. But I charge you, considering what you carry and what you are endowed with, you must do these things. It is a continuous practice that will help you hold on to the torch of healing that you have found.

> " *We lie to ourselves about what is going on because we do not want to address what we are doing wrong.*

Journey through to assume a state of newness that amplifies your healing voice. I have found that the truth is a powerful

Journey through to assume a state of newness that amplifies your healing voice **"** thing, and when we give it room to shine, it obliterates the emblems of fear, hopelessness, and stagnancy that cloud our vision.

The G.O.F.R.E.E framework is designed to initiate a liberating experience. The goal is to unleash a sequence of self reflection that allows you to detach from the past experiences. Let's talk about how the unveiling progresses. It really is a catalyst for liberty. Let's start with the big "G".

G: GRIEVE OVER THE LOSS

Grieve over the loss. Grief naturally follows loss, and you must not stifle it. It is a unique reaction that matters and needs to be acknowledged. Allow yourself to understand the depth of the loss. Permit yourself to articulate what you lost to help you manage your grief. Sometimes it is expressed verbally, through our actions or our responses. The vehicle you choose is up to you but choose it and use it. When you do this, you burst open the prison door, so you can begin to imagine the move forward.

I have often heard it said that you should *"leave the pain behind and move on."* I agree that this approach may work for some, but it was different for me. Contrary to that saying, I chose a different path. Could it be that perhaps we do not leave the pain behind? Instead, I packaged it for the transition. The grieving stage allowed me to package it in an appropriate box so that when I referenced it on- my journey forward, it was no longer a showstopper. It became a decision enhancer. It became an aid for reflection at every inflection point. It gave a strong spring to my pivot.

In reflection, I will share this with you. It is so critical to frame the experience. Don't allow it to seep into all dimensions of your life and boomerang back to you with falsehood. Remember, the grief is for "a thing lost" and not for "all things lost." Make sure you put the extent of the loss into perspective. The loss applies to a specific thing, a person, a moment, or even an event. Don't generalize it! In the absence of this mental exercise, the emotional perception that *"all is lost"* will persist.

Remember, the grief is for "a thing lost" and not for "all things lost."

You have greatness not only inside of you but ahead of you, waiting to be unleashed. Your eternal grieving is a shackle suffocating its release.

I agree that every loss demands a time of attention to grieving, and it is crucial to allow yourself the time to do so. You may, however, ask the question, *"How long is long enough"*? Sorry to burst your bubble, but I cannot answer that question. Every single one of us is different. I can point you to something that will help you expedite the process, and it is this: You have greatness not only inside of you but ahead of you, waiting to be unleashed. Your eternal grieving is a shackle suffocating its release.

O: ORIENT YOURSELF QUICKLY

Okay, let's get our bearings right! It's now time for the realization of where you are. Do you know something?

When the tears are streaming down your face, and your heart is humming on autopilot, it is easy to lose sight of where you are heading. I know it hurts but wipe your tears and open your eyes long enough to familiarize yourself with where you are. Ask yourself the question of your location and destination. *"Where am I now, and where am I heading? What do I have to do to get there?"* In your assessment, keep this fact in mind: orientation is essentially the determination of the relative position of something or someone. It is an introduction and an adjustment to a new environment or a new norm. When the location is confirmed, there is always a matter of recalibrating to acknowledge what remains.

So, as you recalibrate, remember this fundamental truth and work your way from there. What remains is you, the being God created, and the thing that He empowered you with for your Kingdom purpose. Process this reminder as a matter of urgency. It is an anchor that will position you to pivot to the truth of who you are and what lies ahead.

It is only challenging because there is an inevitable confrontation with many things that happened

You have to invest the time to sort through, differentiate between, and categorize them to help you with the next step of forgiving. This process may seem like a daunting task and lend itself to procrastination. That is to be expected. It is only challenging because there is an inevitable confrontation with many things that happened. But, if you allow yourself to journey through, it will work well for you. It will allow you to detangle yourself from the claws of confusion and delusion one truth at a time. Remember, you have a ton of information spanning realms of the physical, mental, emotional, and spiritual.

It may not feel like it but getting through this phase will help you immensely in your journey forward. The process is a powerful catalyst for freedom and will pivot you to your new place and space. As you navigate through it, your belief system will become reconfigured and will orient you in your truth anchors.

F: FORGIVE UNCONDITIONALLY

If you have made it this far, let me give you a virtual pat on the back because you have come a long way. Well done! Now let the progress continue. It's time to shed all and any unnecessary weight.

> *"Wherefore seeing we also are compassed about with so great a cloud of witnesses, let us lay aside every weight, and the sin which doth so easily beset us, and let us run with patience the race that is set before us,".*

Hebrews 12:1 [KJV]

The most counterproductive thing you could do at this point is to lie to yourself. That approach does not set you free, and it never does you any good. It only stamps permanency unto temporary emotional markers. You now know where you are and who you are. Grieving and orienting has laid the groundwork for you to garner up enough courage to forgive with specificity. Identify the things that you need to forgive. Be specific about what and who has to be forgiven if applicable. It is now time to take the lid off and get in there. Go for the kill because the suppressed anger and bitterness only breeds unforgiveness. Don't forget to forgive yourself while you are at it.

Forgive The Offender

So much has been said and done and, understandably, anger, bitterness, and perhaps hatred exists. In Genesis 50:15-20, we see the brothers' expectation of Joseph's reaction to their deeds and then get to marvel at his actual response. I know for sure that the offender always expects the worst of you because, in their mind, that is the measure of response they would probably give to the situation. Your forgiveness certainly disarms the offender. Don't accentuate what needs to be diminished and vice versa, See the offender through God's eyes; in all their humanity and let it go.

Give It To Get It

Let's start by processing this Scripture to anchor us. *"For if you forgive men their trespasses, your heavenly Father will also forgive you. But if you do not forgive men their trespasses, neither will your Father forgive your trespasses"* (Matthew 6: 14-15 NKJV). It is hard to take it all in, but that is the requirement. When we hold on to offenses, we hurt ourselves. The truth is, your life's on the line here, and this should be a no brainer. But is it? No! It's not because it is contrary to our preferred behavior. God is open as long as we open up to let go and trust Him to work it out on our behalf. Not easy, but necessary.

The process of forgiving allows you to identify what hurts you. Once you recognize it, you then have to position yourself to see things from Christ's angle. This angle will enable you to reflect on what He has done for you and how He has allowed you back in after all your mess and imperfections.

Humility

I think humility is more comfortable to talk about than it is to exercise. Through this phase, my process helped me extend grace and show mercy but not before examining myself. I had to strip down to the lowest level of similarity between myself and the offender. At that level, you see yourself in all your imperfection and ugliness. If you glance over to look at the offender, you will find that you look alike. The similarity may not be exact but it is certainly similar. You may have varying degrees of disgusting ugliness, but it is there and it will surely humble you.

I recall how grace and mercy partnered as a singular voice to remind me of all the undeserving saves God had afforded me. You could refuse to bend, but it's hard to do when you acknowledge your own ugliness. It will help to remember what God says in His Word. *"So, as those who have been chosen of God, holy and beloved, put on a heart of compassion, kindness, humility, gentleness, and patience; bearing with one another, and forgiving each other, whoever has a complaint against anyone; just as the Lord forgave you, so also should you." -Colossians 3:12-13 (NASB)*

Holy Spirit, Help Me!

I know it is hard to forgive, but I also know it has to happen quickly for your survival. You need it to function. While God expects us to do what He asks of us in His Word, He does not leave us helpless. Jesus came and showed the example of forgiveness and then sent the Holy Spirit after that. If you find it difficult to let go, call on the Holy Spirit to help you and clothe you with humility and mercy. Take the leap and trust Him to work it out to nurture everyone's good.

Forgiving is hard, but it lightens your load and removes the weight and burden of bitterness, discontentment, and ill will. It is the most freeing thing you could ever do for yourself! Know this; unforgiveness is the biggest thief of time. It is a prison, and the sooner you forgive the offender, the better it will be for your soul. As my Pastor always says, unforgiveness is like drinking poison and expecting the other person to die. Forgive yourself and forgive the other person. Yes, yes, you may feel like they don't deserve it, but the truth is we owe it to them even if they don't ask for it. Remember, forgiveness precedes love, so do it and then be in expectation.

R: RELEASE THEM FROM YOUR HEART

In a moment of reflection, I find it uncontrollably hilarious that I tolerated the residence of a tenant who did not want to live in my building. Why was I holding on to something and someone that wanted me to let them go? I think it is utterly irresponsible to allow someone to take residence in a vessel like yourself. When you release a thing, you have to open up where it resides to give it an outlet.

God is asking us to release them so we can be released. Not that easy, is it? But remember that releasing them allows you to move along in your journey of becoming. I know the idea of holding on is attractive and satisfying. I would like to hold on too, but it is too expensive for me to do so. I don't know about you, but that is a price I am not willing to pay. I have spent enough already. Release them from your heart if you want to wave the forgiveness card in truth and inspire others. If you have forgiven them, let it go. Be careful here because if you see the signs of bitterness sneak in, you need to pause and check yourself. They are disappointment, anger, resentment and multiple layers of emotion you will recognize as toxic. These signs are evidence of unforgiveness. You have to forgive to be able to release them from your heart. When you forgive, you allow yourself to see them in a new light and a new narrative that you now control.

E: EMBRACE WHAT LIES AHEAD

Open hands have room to receive and to carry. Embracing requires readiness, openness, willingness, and space. Enthusiasm does not necessarily mean you are willing, but rather, it puts you in place, closer to anticipation. It is your state of being as a result of all the work you have done. Willingness, on the other hand, requires a desire. The desire is what will open you up to execute. In the journey forward, it is crucial to let go and embrace what lies ahead.

To embrace, you have to be open and unloaded. Unloaded because it is hard to take in anything when you are full. It is hard to hold on to something when you are still holding so much. The journey needs you to shed some things that may be weighing you down.

Allow yourself to see ahead and explore all the possibilities. It feels comfortable to sit in what you see around you. This place may feel comfortable, but it is costly. Let go and move on to the untold. Embrace your future and allow hope to manifest her evidence. There is so much more ahead, and your future is bright indeed.

E: EXPERIENCE BY PARTICIPATING

Anyone can be oblivious and cruise on autopilot. You are not anyone; you are someone. It is possible to be on autopilot and not realize it. The fact is, if you're going to have an experience, you have to participate. An experience demands participation.

Being an observer is easy but participation unleashes discovery. This is a chance to " discover who you are after the traumatic experience. Do it!

Recollection is a powerful thing. When faced with a situation, you withdraw reference points from your experiences. I have thought about it and intentionally observed myself in the process. You will be presented with many options when you exit from your experiences. It is like a menu to select from. You can decide to be intentional about what you choose out of the lot. Once chosen, you have to decide how you will position it now that it is separated from the others. Many things will come to mind but decide to participate in what funds your peace and allows you to flourish.

If you are going to enjoy the experience, you have to exert some energy through participation. Make the most of your involvement and investment. Being an observer is easy but participation unleashes discovery. This is a chance to discover who you are after the traumatic experience. Do it!

Healing Ambassador License
- Elle Mills

> *Star so bright, shine so bright,*
> *Life so bright, rise to fight!*
> *The Torch of Life*
> *It stays bright*
> *by God's breath which fans its light*
>
> *I am she who walks the path*
> *I am she who chose this life*
> *This life to glorify the One True God*
> *So, watch my back and see my core*
>
> *I am stopping for no one*
> *Oh No! Not anymore*
> *I got it stamped, and I am dangerous.*
> *This healing torch is mine to fly*
>
> *Come rain or scorch*
> *That too is fine*
> *Cause I will not lose my license*
> *No not I*
> *My healing ambassador license*
> *Yes, this is mine to fly*

HEALING AMBASSADOR

This certifies that

_____

HAS EARNED THE CREDIT TO PASS ON THE HEALING TORCH

*"Dear friend, I pray that you may enjoy good health
and that all may go well with you, even as your soul
is getting along well."*

Hebrews 12:1 [KJV]

The Good News: A pure soul is one that not only wishes wellness on himself, but also on others.

CHAPTER NINE

Tapestry-Eureka-Ecclesia!

"For I know the plans I have for you", declares the Lord, "plans to prosper you and not harm you, plans to give you hope and a future."

Jeremiah 29:11 [NIV]

It happened suddenly, and it was my eureka moment when I clearly understood. It was an "Aha!" moment when the scripture above became a lighthouse beckoning to me and championing my focus.

I could hear the direction to proceed. I was no longer muted nor engulfed by the solitude of an inner interview to discount the possibility of God's boundless ability. I could hear the singular life promise to walk in His way and in pursuit of His truth to unlock the life that was slowly seeping out. This was the beginning of the end!

The path was structured to get me to God. A series of encounters enveloped my existence and brought clarity to the way of being in the Lord through His Word. To get to God, I had to acknowledge Him and His infinite ability. I could not get to Him if I did not believe that He was there. Out of the acknowledgment of His existence came the dependence on Him. So did the unfathomable depth of understanding of the acutely critical need for a relationship with Him. My SOS was registered on this journey and attended to with a swift rescue of a promised life.

You see, God has plans for me. As far as I understood, a minimal requirement for a plan is intent. If God has plans for me, then He has an intention. This intention requires effort, and effort involves interest. Now here was the faith step. Interest requires one of two things, love or hate. The outcome of the plan determines the source or reason for the appeal. Because I know God is love, I can rest assured that the goal is to prosper and bring me to an expected end.

I began to wonder about what else was possible. The security in knowing there is someone who is orchestrating all things to yield my prosperity was priceless. The restoration slowly but surely manifested in multiple areas of my life. It felt like I had walked up to and opened gates of discovery and stepped into dimensions of the God of impossibilities and His infinite abilities. As it gracefully unfolded, I marveled, and I soon realized that the best is undoubtedly yet to come.

I had been pushed into an uncomfortable space and had to find comfort in Him to remain alive. It was a long road that called for a rewiring of my mind, and He found His servant to guide me. This phase required divinely assigned shepherds to guide me through. My shepherds, Pastors Joe and Eunice Asmah held my hand through this phase, and God ensured that my story progressed in His plan. Like those at the gate called Beautiful, I was at the House of Restoration. I am sincerely grateful to God for the All Nations Church NJ ministry.

I found and followed God's way; I connected to Him and gradually understood why all this was necessary. By aligning with God's truth, I tapped into life, clarity, and possibility.

CHAPTER TEN

Conclusion

Transitions are not fun, but it is critically important to embrace the swift movement from victim to victor and Kingdom enforcer. The advancement through is the antidote against stagnancy. The man who left you stranded in the marriage journey is just that; a man. Just because he (man) could not work with you does not mean HE (God) cannot work with you. God has endowed each one of us with a Kingdom purpose that surpasses offense, disappointment, or complacency, among other things. My journey taught me that I have a responsibility to deliver and execute my God's purpose. You are the only one who can achieve your purpose.

Transitions are not fun, but it is critically important to **"** *embrace the swift movement from victim to victor and Kingdom enforcer*

You were created, encapsulated, and incubated with all that is needed to accomplish that purpose. While I wished for a time that I would be exempt from delivering my purpose, I quickly embraced the fact that it does not get diluted because I was disappointed by a man. God expects

You were created, encapsulated, and **"** *incubated with all that is needed to accomplish that purpose.*

that we will number our days assigned to accomplish His will and passionately pursue without delay the enforcement of the Kingdom's purpose on earth as it is in heaven. My prayer then shifted to solicit Kingdom resources to learn to number my days and do the will of God, which was very much the opposite of my preferred choice for execution.

You are a woman who champions the manifestation of the sons of God. The earth is looking to you as the custodian of the vessels of God, the children God blessed you with. You are a wonder, a creation of the Almighty to reflect His cuddle and release. His word in Jeremiah 1:5 NLT states that *"I knew you before I formed you in your mother's womb. Before you were born I set you apart and appointed you as my prophet to the nations.."* There is a treasure in the earthen vessel that you must nurture to be released.

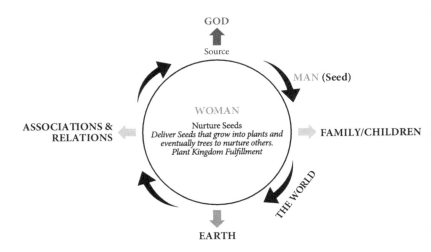

Let us underscore the interdependencies on each other. I need you and you need me. You may be one degree or several removed from me but one thing is true; we are connected. God is the Source for all and He saw it fit to connect us. In the marriage journey, God blesses the union in several ways, some with children. The seed that manifests into a child may have come from the man you no longer call husband, but remember it originated from God, the Source. So if that be the case, you are not exempt from nurturing that seed to grow into a Kingdom enforcer.

When the angel came to Mary and announced that she would be found with seed, Joseph had a choice. He could have decided that this was not part of his plan and moved on. If that had been the case, I believe Jesus would have still been born and been nurtured to fulfill His purpose. All I am saying is, do not quit because a man left you, but rather press on because God has got you. The man was only a conduit for God. And as you nurture what He has given you, remember the impact on other families and children through the natural connections of our ecosystem. What you breathed into yours from your place of healing will make our collective work easier. However, if you feed these ones from a place of bitterness, you lay a foundation for the world to further corrupt.

I conclude with this. There are three sides to the marriage aisle – Those entering, those in it, and those contemplating an exit. I hope I have given you things to consider in your longing for either of the three sides of the aisle.

The divorce path is one that I wish was less travelled. Unfortunately, this is not the case. So, it remains that your individual decisions reverberate through generations.

There is a place of empathy that assists the pause that's necessary for reflection. Don't trade twenty minutes of empathy for a lifetime of misery. Allow yourself to take a pause instead of throwing a word punch your partner will likely not recover from. Don't let a temporary offense gain an enduring influence. After all, we are here to live life and not live marriage. So, let life happen in your union. Selah.

Bibliography

1. Editor. "Musculoskeletal Archives - Medical Art Library." Medical Art Library, https://medicalartlibrary.com/category/musculoskeletal/. Accessed 22 Jan. 2021.

2. Work, Theology. "God Created Woman as an Ezer Kind of Helper (Genesis 2:18) | Article | Theology of Work." Theology of Work | What Does the Bible Say About Faith and Work?, https://www.theologyofwork.org/key-topics/women-and-work-in-the-old-testament/god-created-woman-as-an-ezer-kind-of-helper-genesis-218. Accessed 22 Jan. 2021.

3. "H5828 - `ezer - Strong's Hebrew Lexicon (KJV)." Blue Letter Bible, https://www.blueletterbible.org/lang/lexicon/lexicon.cfm?t=kjv&strongs=h5828. Accessed 31 Jan. 2021.

4. Hookedondriving. Flags, The Key to Your Safety: Hooked On Driving. YouTube, 15 Apr. 2010, https://www.youtube.com/watch?v=K68cilr3TnA.

About the Author

Elle is a passionate and purpose-driven daughter of God. She is a facilitator, catalyst and advocate for change. She is the founder of the myladderyourelevator platform, a discovery, growth and healing space activated to nurture courageous conversations that direct us back to God and our Kingdom purpose.

Elle has a passion for Organizational Administration and Development. She is a thought translator and has created several strategic frameworks to crystallize organizational vision. Elle also develops training programs (mentoring, coaching, administration etc.) in support of church systems.

With over 15 years of experience in Human Resources, she has worked with several Fortune 500 companies, partnering with her clients to bring robust HR solutions to their business.

She believes everyone has a unique contribution to make and she pursues opportunities to do just that. Elle is a single mother of three loving, curious and resilient children who bring her the greatest joy and inspiration. She enjoys writing poetry, singing and reading.

Here is how you can connect with her.

- 🌐 www.elleamills.com
- 🌐 www.myladderyourelevator.com
- 🔘 myladderyourelevator
- 🔵 myladderyourelevator
- 🔵 Group: The Huddle Room-my.ladder.your.elevator

Made in the USA
Middletown, DE
30 April 2022